• • • • ▬ • •

Hair Pings

Tweets

& My Status

A Beginner's Guide to

Social Media

• • • • • • •

Authored by: Alfredo Kierszman
Designed by: Brenda L. Ranero

Dedicated to my mom, Ines, for telling me that I was too rough and needed hair school to soften me up. To my wife, Brenda, for her unconditional love and support no matter how many times I change my mind. To my mother in law, Laura, that teaches me more about tolerance, love, and support than she will ever know. Last but not least, love to my 2 monkeys, Angelique and Giovanni, who I love very much.

Please be free and feel free to express your creativity, your love, your talent, your humor, your ideas, and your thoughts. Have peace in your hearts and love for others, always.

>!<

Forward

Who is Tabitha, or Kim Vo, Robert Cromeons, or Richard Thompson? Who are you and who am I, you ask? We are who the T.V., the Radio, the Internet, or the Newspapers say we are. You are the product of what the public eye perceives you to be...Social media can be a tool for building your career. Understanding how the influencer's view of a service or its provider through the use of Social Networking and Social Media will be what we as a society perceives to be socially acceptable for everything that we buy or consume.....within the pages of this book you will find everything you need to begin your journey through your career in the beauty industry by drawing attention to the positive things that have influenced it's author and will hopefully inspire you to take your career from beyond the ordinary, to the couture!

-Stephen Soto Master Stylist

About the Author

Alfredo Kierszman

With his innovation and unique eye for fashion, Alfredo is a highly recognized hair and fashion stylist. Since 1989, Alfredo has been a Stylist, Salon Owner and Industry Educator. He has worked for companies like Sebastian, Paul Mitchell, Nioxin, and currently with Alfaparf Milano. Throughout his career he has worked in every segment of the beauty industry from traditional services to specialized hair replacement and image consultant. A master of his craft he is a sought after educator and speaker to community and industry events. He has received honors from the National Cosmetologist Association and has been granted the role of Facilitating for the American Cancer Society's Look Good Feel Better Programs in which he has participated since 1993. As a highly skilled cosmetologist, he has been featured in various magazines, his editorial work includes writing articles for and have pictorial in American Salon, International Bride, and Ego magazines.

Overview

A little about my tips and bits:

The tips and bits in this book are meant to be 3 fold; first to inspire, second to learn, and third and most importantly to laugh. So please, enjoy, because to not enjoy this book and more importantly the Beauty industry, would not give any justice to the purpose for which it was written.

A little about pings, tweets and my status:

I use social web site platforms to communicate with my audience, clients and circle of influence. I share them with you for kicks. You will see that they have no rhyme or reason to the unsuspecting, but for you, pings, will help keep you in front of your clients, potential clients, and new clients, and so on, you will grow. **Just you try not to**.

A little about Social marketing:

Listening to your customers and getting to know their influencers can have a profound affect on how quickly your business will grow and how it will best succeed. Sites like Myspace, Facebook, Twitter, Linkedin, or your use of blogs, are the platforms people are using to share their thoughts and converse about those influences. To not use the internet for marketing and more importantly for networking

Is not an option anymore; it is essential for marketing to every age demographic.

Sin Qua Nons, a Latin phrase meaning the absolutely essential things. I decided to add portions of this book because we need it. My client and friend for many years, David Walke, wrote the manuscript called Sin Qua Nons "Some of Life's Essentials" (and other stuff, too) He has dedicated it to his children D. Martin Walke & Lauren E. Walke.

One day while I was cutting David's hair he told me he had written the book and told me a bit about it. I asked him to share it with me and he graciously gave me a copy. Wow, what a book, filled with so many values important for living. It impressed me to share something from the book weekly with my family.

In his words:

"This information that I have accumulated over many years is not new or novel but it is intended to illustrate a lesson or convey a truth."

Table of Contents

**This book is for Hair Stylists,
            the Challenged Driven**

• • • • • • •

Join my socials at

www.HairByAlfredo.com

• • • • • • •

• • • • • • •

The Hair

The Cuticle is the outside layer of the hair shaft.

The Cortex is the mid-layer of the hair shaft. Strength, elasticity, and size are functions of the cortex.

The Matrix is the middle portion of the hair shaft. The Matrix is rich in the sulphur-containing amino acid cystine.

Made you think… lol

• • • • • • •

• • • • • • •

Hair ∼

It is actually dead material when it leaves its root - otherwise it would hurt very much when your hairdresser works with their scissors.

• • • • • • •

• • • • • • •

The average scalp has
100,000 strands,
or
just fewer than 1,000 per
square inch

• • • • • • •

We are born with all our hair follicles.

Some are programmed to grow pigmented hair (as on our scalp) up to 3 feet in length.

• • • • • • •

Hair loss in men can start
as early as

PUBERTY.

• • • • • • •

• • • • • • •

Newspaper
Advertisement Wanted:
Hair cutter. Excellent
growth potential ☺

• • • • • •

• • • • • • •

Patient: My hair keeps falling out. What can you give me to keep it in? ☺

Doctor: A shoebox.

• • • • • • •

• • • • • • •

Are hair websites located on mane frames? :)

So let's get online with social marketing.
Do this first: Get a

- Username
- Company name
- Logo
- Profile picture
- Quote
- Domain name

• • • • • • •

• • • • • • •

Social media and social marketing are very powerful stuff. The power of social media is the ability to reach people. People you may not have easily reached before the internet. Anyone from any country can view information on the web, even the shy ones.

People today want to do business with professionals they know, trust and are qualified. Having web articles, blogs, a fan page, groups, friends, and followers makes you credible.

• • • • • • •

• • • • • • •

**Accept
a breath mint
if someone
offers you one.**

• • • • • • •

• • • • • • •

Don't be lazy. If you don't like what you just did to your client's hair, why should they? Just fix it. Apologize, and give them a % off for wasting their time. You may gain a client for life and more importantly a friend.

• • • • • • •

• • • • • • •

Put a band-aid on.

Blood will show

on   the   high   lights…   lol

• • • • • • •

13

• • • • • • •

The Primary colors are still **BLUE, RED,**

AND YELLOW

The secondary colors are formed by mixing

equal part of the primary colors.

Blue and yellow = Green (aren't you GLAD)

Blue and red = Violet (yes purple)

Red and Yellow = Orange (or copper)

• • • • • • •

• • • • • • •

Warm colors - **RED, ORANGE, YELLOW**

Cool colors - **GREEN, BLUE, VIOLET**

Just as a reminder

The cool color that is opposite the warm color will neutralize it and vice versa.

So instead of running like a mad man to the color wheel in the back room

Stop- Drop- and Roll

No really stop ask yourself

What is the missing…

• • • • • • •

• • • • • • •

PRIMARY COLOR

• • • • • • •

● ● ● ● ● ● ●

Florescent lights – put out cool tonal reflections
Standard lights – put out warm tonal reflections
Sunlight light – is a perfect light reflecting both
cool and warm tones

>!<   >!<

● ● ● ● ● ● ●

• • • • • • •

In this industry you are constantly repopulating yourself. Constantly looking for and creating loyal followers to your business.

Bodies in your chairs

• • • • • • •

• • • • • • •

How will you market to them?

How will you meet them?

How will you get those bodies in your chair?

• • • • • • •

• • • • • • •

Network Marketing
and now more
importantly
Social Networking

• • • • • • •

• • • • • • •

Network Marketing is the term that describes a marketing structure used by many companies as a part of their overall marketing strategy. The structure is designed to create a marketing & sales force of promoters that are loyal to the brand and rewards them for it. It is also known as relationship referral and word of mouth marketing. **You are the company and your clients the promoters.**

• • • • • • •

• • • • • • •

Set yourself apart by offering convenience, and free style evaluations.

• • • • • • •

• • • • • • •

Luck favors the prepared man.

(Chance favors the prepared mind.)

"Louis Pasteur
French chemist & biologist"

• • • • • • •

• • • • • • •

When
selling
yourself
under
promise
and
over
deliver.

• • • • • • •

● ● ● ● ● ● ●

Style Evaluation

1. On a scale of 1 to 10 how much do you like your hair?

2. On that same scale. How much do you like the length?

3. Why?

4. How much do you like the color?

5. Why?

6. In the past, was there a time that you liked your hair the best?

7. Why?

8. If I had a wand and I could do anything with your hair, what would it be?

9. Six months from today it will be _____ how would you like you're hair to look then?

10. What were you hoping we could do for you today?

● ● ● ● ● ● ●

• • • • • • •

Give to a worthy cause.
Not just your $ but your
time and talent as well
I like the
American Cancer
Society's Look Good…
Feel Better ☺

www.lgfb.com

• • • • • • •

• • • • • • •

**Never
say anything
uncomplimentary about
someone else's work.**

**You will always look
worse.**

• • • • • • •

• • • • • • •

You want to talk to your client about something? Here is a topic of conversation

Products and usage / rebooking for maintenance

• • • • • • •

• • • • • • •

**A hand-written
thank you note is always
better received.
So,**

Thank you

• • • • • • •

• • • • • • •

Know this before you color someone's hair.

   A. Their starting color (natural and/or cosmetic)

   B. The desired hair color

   C. The texture of the hair

   D. The porosity of the hair

   E. The contributing underlying pigment

   F. The product being used.

• • • • • • •

• • • • • • •

Hair color does not lift
hair color.
Contrasti does

• • • • • • •

Purification or
Color Extraction

Never- stripping, glamour bath,
or soap cap.

• • • • • • •

• • • • • • •

What is the potential client's incentive for coming in to the salon?

A Free Style Evaluation

• • • • • • •

• • • • • • •

**Save time
for goodness sakes just fill
the hair if you have too.**

Oh yeah – Repigmentize

• • • • • • •

• • • • • • •

Why does color fade?

You shampoo your hair.

• • • • • • •

• • • • • • •

And

Sunlight and florescent lights

Oh yeah over the counter color products that have color pigments the size of tennis balls, and the use crappy shampoo. Which are all big no no's.

Should I keep on going?

• • • • • • •

Driving website traffic

I can tell you from my own experience regarding the increase of traffic to my website.

I had my website up and running and it looked good. But no one was visiting it. I know this because I linked my website to Google Analytics which is a must do. Here and there I would have visits but not very many. One day, out of the blue, I had like 10 visits. Wow, I was so excited. My friend said "ok now check out the full report to see where those visits came from". As it turns out, I had 2 unique views but the rest were from me showing it to people. Lol

By this time I was very frustrated. I was so proud of my website and I wanted people to visit it. I told all my facebook friends and my clients but still nothing.

●　●　●　●　●　●　●

(Stage right enters)

Joel Goldstein

●　●　●　●　●　●　●

● ● ● ● ● ● ●

Joel is a very down to earth guy that I first met at a networking meet up. He spoke about the importance of social media and some social networking thing. I didn't understand but with blind ambition I listened and decided to try. I thought to myself, what can I lose anyway? So on my downtime at the salon, which we all have, I tried some of what Joel said, to the best of my limited ability of course.

Oh, did I mention Joel was nominated at 24 for Entrepreneur of the Year, he is a professional speaker, an internet marketing consultant, he has been featured on TV in newspapers and magazines, he is an expert in internet marketing strategies and an author i.e.
A Professional's Guide to Social Media (Reach 550 Million Potential clients)

● ● ● ● ● ● ●

• • • • • • •

So in short, this is what I got from what Joel said. BTW – I am not a computer savvy person so it was a bit scary. He did inspire me to let my

Nerd Flag Fly.

Wow, how liberating!

I know that I have just scratched the surface but here it goes.
I now share with you.

• • • • • • •

• • • • • • •

Set up your PROFESSIONAL social sites, that's right, professional, if you have not already. The one with a picture of your cute dog is great. But what I'm speaking about is one with a good picture of you, the hair stylist, and the style authority in their life.
Some ideas are:

Facebook.com

Myspace.com

Twitter.com

Linkedin.com

Classmates.com

Myyearbook.com

Livejournal.com

Imeen.com

Bebo.com

Google.com/buzz

• • • • • • •

● ● ● ● ● ● ●

I could go on and on, so pick some, or all, set yourself up.

After I set myself up with a few I then went to...

...Wait for it.

● ● ● ● ● ●

• • • • • • •

Wait for it.

• • • • • • •

• • • • • • •

Wait for it.

• • • • • • •

• • • • • • •

Ping.fm

now you can also use Socialposter.com

but I used Ping.fm

• • • • • • •

• • • • • • •

First I signed up

Second linked my socials to it

Then I got my ping.fm cell number which allows me to up-date my ping status via text (There is a patent pending app. for mobile devices)

And Finally...Like Magic!

• • • • • • •

Ping

Whatever you send to your ping status gets sent to all of your other social sites – Ping.

:) Good Stuff

• • • • • • •

Did you get that?

Update all of you social sites from 1 site!!!!

Yeah, I'm excited. No more going from site to

site just to say…

I am grumpy.

• • • • • • •

• • • • • • •

Ping.fm is a simple and free service that makes updating your social networks a snap. Post from anywhere, to anywhere.

Then there is Hootsuite.com this site allows for you to manage multiple social sites on one site.

So all this work, what is in it for you?

This allows you to be credible and an authority of your industry within your circle of influence. You are also creating a larger circle of influence and the bottom line principle here is…

• • • • • • •

• • • • • • •

**The level of your success
is solely based on the #
of people you put your
products or service
in front of.**

(read it again if you need to and let it settle)

• • • • • • •

• • • • • • •

This way you are constantly in the mind of your clients and potential client.
And it's all FREE!!!

• • • • • • •

• • • • • • •

**Plan your work
and
work your plan.**

● ● ● ● ● ● ●

The Social Media Shift

Hair Stylists have always been a social industry, it is part of our culture. The game changer is the web and the many new platforms of Social media.

Paul Gillin Author of The Secrets of Social Media Marketing says "Social Media will alter our lives and institutions in ways we are only beginning to comprehend. More then 75% of the U.S. adult population is now online. By 2012 we will be sharing our experiences, observations, opinions with a global audience as freely as we pick up the phone today."

Some people still believe that social media is a fad, a bubble that will burst as suddenly and dramatically as the first internet bubble did. They are very wrong.

Social media is not about multimillion dollar corporations making multimillions of dollars. Social media is about ordinary people taking control of the world around them and finding creative new ways to bring their collective voice together to get what they want.

The stunning speed in which these changes are occurring has blindsided business marketers. The C.E.O.'s and C.F.O. and all the other head Officers now have to become C.C.O.'s "Chief Conversation Officers."

● ● ● ● ● ● ●

● ● ● ● ● ● ●

The Salon Reception Shift

I won't go into to much details but I will say this regarding the Salon Receptionist. Over the years, we have looked for ways to justify their economic existence in the salon. With out a doubt the Beauty industry is different. We don't typically hire summer help unless you have a salon in the Hampton or some other vacation destination of the sort, because most salons have a slow down in business during the summer months.

After the summer, we end up hiring either one of our client / housewives that needs to get out of the house for a few hours a day or a high school student that needs a part time job. Then, we struggle to train them to answer the phone and book our appointments.

If we want and can spend a little more money, we hire a more qualified person, and call them "Salon Coordinator" or "Salon Manager", but in the end they still struggle to answer the phone, make appointments, and greet guest. Then we still ask them to do towels, sweep, and keep the salons appearances. Lol

So, the challenges are our expectations not their abilities.

● ● ● ● ● ● ●

● ● ● ● ● ● ●

We think of our moms' salons and our grandmothers salon's with twice as many clients, twice as many stylist working, none of the luxuries of today and a receptionist who made half the money and got twice as much done. How is that even possible?

Easy, we are under utilizing the intelligence of today's generation and say they don't have work ethics. I personally witnessed an 18 year old girl single handedly take over a salon that was dead after 10 years of professional stylist running it the old fashion way and make a success of it. Why and how? She did not understand anything about the way it was done she only knew how it should be done.

Do not hire a receptionist, A salon manager, or a salon coordinator; try this on for size, hire instead, A "Social Marketing Specialist" that manages all of the salons social networking platforms including replying and posting blogs while also making online, texting, and phone appointments. Oh yeah and sweeps and folds towels, and greets the real live guest to the salon. The title alone will make them a better worker. They will pleasantly surprise you.

● ● ● ● ● ● ●

• • • • • • •

And they go to

High School!

:)

• • • • • • •

• • • • • • •

Know your facts, but remember it's passion that persuades.

• • • • • • •

• • • • • • •

If you own the Salon, dress better than your staff and coworkers.

Stylist dress better than your clients.

• • • • • • •

• • • • • • •

Find and have a good mentor.

Become a good mentor.

• • • • • • •

**Learn the right way
before
you learn the short cuts.**

• • • • • • •

• • • • • • •

Cut on purpose.

• • • • • • •

• • • • • • •

Sweep some.

• • • • • • •

• • • • • •

Then sweep some
more.

Please and
thank you.

• • • • • •

• • • • • • •

Be a Team Player
&
Help clean the
salon.

Please and thank you!

:)

• • • • • • •

• • • • • • •

**To add dimension
to blondes
add low lights**

that are 2 levels deeper.

• • • • • • •

● ● ● ● ● ● ●

The Level System

1. Black
2. Darkest Brown
3. Dark Brown
4. Medium Brown
5. Light Brown
6. Dark Blonde
7. Medium Blonde
8. Light Blonde
9. Very Light Blonde
10. Lightest Blonde
11.
12.
13. Blonde orexcia

Inform your guest.

● ● ● ● ● ● ●

● ● ● ● ● ● ●

Potential client- How much for a trim?

Stylist - $55.

Potential client – For a trim! I don't want a hair cut. I just want a trim.

Stylist – I charge for what I leave on not what I take off.

NEW CLIENT – Oh I see. ☺

● ● ● ● ● ● ●

• • • • • • •

Cut every color
and
color every cut.

• • • • • • •

• • • • • • •

Use the appropriate developer for the brand of color that you are using.

• • • • • • •

Use 10 volume as often as you can.

Only use 20 volume for on the scalp bleach. No matter what your client says.

• • • • • • •

When in doubt ask a colleague.

If you are both in doubt, call the product hot line. Most product have one.   If they don't have a hot line,

DON'T USE THE PRODUCT.
Alfredo Kierszman

• • • • • • •

• • • • • • •

Rule of thumb

Developer = Peroxide or H_2O_2 / Results

10 vol. = 3% deposit only/ tone on tone

20 vol. = 6% gray coverage/ 1 level of lift

30 vol. = 9% gray coverage / 2 levels of lift

40 vol. = 12% gray coverage / 3 levels of lift

To get 5 levels of lift use extra lightning

cream or a boosting catalyst.

If you need more than 5 levels of lift

DECOLORIZE

• • • • • • •

• • • • • • •

Always use a Barrier Cream when coloring hair.

Apply with cotton, a Q-tip, or a brush.

Never your fingers.

Your client's salon visit should always be their experience.

You are there to deliver it.

If they want quiet… be quiet.

If they want fun… be fun.

But remember they always want to relax; it is there time not yours.

• • • • • • •

• • • • • • •

What does a blonde call a bottle of black hair dye?

Artificial intelligence. ☺

• • • • • • •

• • • • • • •

Yeah you've thought this at least once

If you want a new look, I'll work hard to make you happy and I'll want you to like it. After you leave my salon, I'll worry about what you think. You see I work on people, not on cars on an assembly line. And if by chance you feel like calling to tell me how happy you are with my work, you will make me smile.

• • • • • • •

· · · · · · ·

When a client says they're in a rush, I tell them they need to schedule their time better. My work takes time…lol

Think this… but say something like…

I will be as efficient as I can but I'm sure you do not want me to rush. If they are getting color, one can reply with…

I will be as efficient as I can but your color has its own processing time and I can not rush it or it will not work. Sorry

· · · · · · ·

• • • • • • •

Re-book your guest every time

• • • • • • •

• • • • • • •

Set daily goals to
achieve.

This moves you into
action.

• • • • • • •

• • • • • • •

Listen to the story   you
tell people about yourself.
Do you like it?

• • • • • • •

• • • • • • •

Change your story,
  Change your reality,
    Change your destiny.

• • • • • • •

• • • • • • •

Changing your present will soon change your past.

"Diane Losoncy"

• • • • • • •

● ● ● ● ● ● ●

The market is saturated with every possible product to make thin hair thick, dull hair shiny, and curly hair straight. But putting too much junk in your hair will almost always kill a look. More is not more. Your hair wants to be healthy. That doesn't mean trying to totally re-create it every day. Just help it a little. Let it do its thing.

● ● ● ● ● ● ●

• • • • • • •

**Congratulate yourself
when you meet a crisis
head on and work
through it.**

• • • • • • •

• • • • • • •

**Read every day
    something to grow on.**

• • • • • • •

• • • • • • •

**Read every day
    something to grow on.**

• • • • • • •

• • • • • • •

Have a personal mission statement.
Write it, memorize it, and tell others.

Mine is:
I live with the concept of constant and never ending improvement or C.A.N.I.

• • • • • • •

• • • • • •

Have a personal motto
– put it on all your
marketing pieces.

Mine is:
Because creativity
      requires brilliance

• • • • • •

• • • • • • •

Do not attempt hairstylist-talk.

Do you really know what "thinning"

or "graduation" mean?

Leave the terminology to the

professionals. ☺

• • • • • • •

• • • • • • •

"The purpose of business is to provide a service to your client, and if you do that well, it will also generate a profit."

Robert J Ciatto
employee since 1954
Johnson & Johnson

• • • • • • •

• • • • • • •

Helpful hints

Do not apply chemical products on damaged or irritated skin. Avoid pre-shampooing

Observe accurate processing time.

• • • • • • •

• • • • • • •

Some people are just too large or their cheeks too round for the style they want. They should look at themselves in the mirror sometime.

• • • • • • •

• • • • • • •

Client will stay nameless.

"My demon is my frizzy hair. STOP IT!"

• • • • • • •

• • • • • • •

**Yes it is true,
getting your hair colored
by a professional can
actually reduce frizz.**

• • • • • • •

• • • • • • •

Just voted – The best business building program available

YOUR BEST WORK.

Need I say more?

• • • • • • •

• • • • • • •

Don't think of it as if

You're fired.

Think of it as if

You're free.

Just saying it happens

• • • • • • •

• • • • • • •

From near to far, from here to there, funny things are everywhere.
Dr. Seuss

In Snow White the Seven Dwarfs names are Sleepy, Grumpy, Happy, Doc, Dopey, Sneezy, and Bashful You never know when you may need to know that bit of info.

• • • • • • •

• • • • • • •

Who is a Success?

That man is a success who has lived well,
laughed often and loved much;
Who has gained the respect of intelligent
men and the love of children;
Who has filled his niche and accomplished
his task;
Who leaves the world better than he found
it, whether by an improved poppy, a perfect
poem, or a rescued soul;
Who never lacked appreciation of earth's
beauty or failed to express it;
Who looked for the best in others and gave
the best he had.

Robert Louis Stevenson

• • • • • • •

● ● ● ● ● ● ●

It's all in a State of Mind

If you think you'll lose- you've lost

For out in the world, you'll find

Success being with a fellow's will,

it's all in the state of mind.

Life's victories don't always go to

the bigger or faster man, but, more

often than not, the man who wins

is the fellow who thinks he can!

● ● ● ● ● ● ●

Be Vigilant

Guard your thoughts –

they become word.

Guard your words –

they become actions.

Guard your actions –

they become habits.

Guard your habits –

they become character.

Guard your character –

it becomes your destiny.

Charles Reade
English Novelist & Dramatist

• • • • • • •

Stay out of the back room for it is
considered the Low Earners Suite

Go out of the salon
if you want to meet new clients

Be behind the chair if you want
to do hair

Alfredo Kierszman

• • • • • • •

• • • • • • •

Take a Class at a
Sassoon Academy

• • • • • • •

• • • • • • •

Follow Trend websites

• • • • • • •

• • • • • • •

Read anything and everything
Beth Minardi

• • • • • • •

• • • • • • •

We cannot comprehend

Joy… until we face sorrow.

Faith… until it is tested.

Peace… until faced with conflict.

Trust… until we are betrayed.

Love… until it is lost.

Hope… until confronted with doubts.

• • • • • • •

• • • • • • •

From Auguries of Innocence

To see a world in a grain of sand

And Heaven in a wild flower,

Hold infinity in the palm of your

hand

And eternity in an hour.

William Blake

• • • • • • •

• • • • • • •

There is less to fear from outside competition than from inside inefficiency, discourtesy, and poor service.

• • • • • • •

• • • • • • •

10/10/80 Personal Finances Plan: Give 10%, Save 10%, and live off the remaining 80%

• • • • • • •

• • • • • • •

**Procrastination is
the assassination of
motivation**

• • • • • • •

Table of liquid measures

3 teaspoons (tsp) = 1 tablespoon (tbsp.)

8 fluid ounces (fl. oz.) = 1 cup (c.)

4 gills = 1 pint

2 cups = 1 pint (pt)

2 pints = 1 quart (qt)

4 quarts = 1 gallon (gal.)

31.5 gallons = 1 barrel

• • • • • • •

Keep away from people who try to belittle your ambitions. Small people always try to do that, but the really great make you feel that you, too, can become great.

Mark Twain

Pain is inevitable; misery is optional.

Vince Lombardi

• • • • • • •

• • • • • • •

There are two ways to color hair

My way and the wrong way

Beth Minardi

• • • • • • •

A good name is much easier kept than recovered.

Thomas Pain

• • • • • • •

No one can make you feel inferior without your consent.

Eleanor Roosevelt

• • • • • • •

● ● ● ● ● ● ●

For of all sad words of tongue or pen,

The saddest are these:

"It might have been!"

**John Greenleaf Whittier,
American poet**

● ● ● ● ● ● ●

• • • • • • •

It's not the load that breaks you, it's the way you carry it.

Lou Holtz

• • • • • • •

• • • • • • •

My wife's friend Diane Nisbett told
her this and I love it.

Never put a
question mark
where God has
put a period.

• • • • • • •

● ● ● ● ● ● ●

Great hair color enhances a person,
everything from her eyes to her skin
tone to her face shape.

Beth Minardi

● ● ● ● ● ● ●

• • • • • • •

The gem cannot be polished without friction, nor a man perfect without trials.

Confucius Chinese philosopher

• • • • • • •

• • • • • • •

Organize and participate in a photo shoot.

Be an assistant of someone in a photo shoot.

• • • • • • •

• • • • • • •

Take at least 4 classes per year that
are industry related.

Take 2 classes a year that are not.

Attend a minimum of 1 International
Beauty Show per year.

Alfredo Kierszman

• • • • • • •

• • • • • • •

If you really want to do something,

you'll find a way.

If you don't, you'll find an excuse.

Will Rogers

• • • • • • •

• • • • • • •

We don't make mistakes

We make discoveries

We don't have challenges

We get opportunities

The Paul Mitchell School

• • • • • • •

• • • • • • •

If you don't have the best of everything, then make the best of everything you have.

Erk Russell

• • • • • • •

• • • • • • •

All that glitters is not gold

Dave Weinbaum

• • • • • • •

• • • • • • •

To help others is to help
yourself.

Max Lucado

• • • • • • •

www.behindthechair.com
Is a good source for
information

• • • • • • •

• • • • • • •

Reading is to the mind what exercise is to the body.

Sir Richard Steel

• • • • • • •

• • • • • • •

To worry is to enjoy a crisis before it happens.

Barbara Johnson, Ph.D.

• • • • • • •

• • • • • • •

Every 4 out of 3 people have trouble with fractions. ☺

The father of every good work is discontent, and its mother is diligence.

Lajos Kassak

• • • • • • •

• • • • • • •

If you give a man a fish, you feed him for a day. If you teach him how to fish you feed him for a lifetime.

• • • • • • •

• • • • • • •

She got her good looks from
her father.
He is a plastic surgeon.

Groucho Marx

• • • • • • •

• • • • • • •

Learn how to cut a proper bob

Learn how to do an up-do

Learn how to say hello to a client

Alfredo Kierszman

• • • • • • •

• • • • • • •

Intelligent people have more zinc
and copper in their hair.

• • • • • • •

● ● ● ● ● ● ●

Excellence is not an act but a habit.
The things you do the most are the
things you will do the best.

Marva Collins

● ● ● ● ● ● ●

Every day, some ordinary person does something extraordinary.

Today it's your turn.

Lou Holtz

Get ready for the X-factor in your life. It is what happens when the line of readiness and the line of opportunity meet.

Seneca
Roman philosopher

• • • • • • •

Take a
Martin Parsons Class

• • • • • • •

• • • • • • •

Honey is the only food that doesn't spoil.

• • • • • • •

• • • • • • •

Success is the ongoing process of striving to become more. The road to success is always under construction. It is a progressive course, not an end to be reached.

Anthony Robbins

• • • • • • •

• • • • • • •

Have you ever seen the deer heads on the walls of a tavern, you know the ones wearing party hats, sunglasses and streamers? I feel sorry for them because they were at the party having a good time And then… ☺

Ellen DeGeneres

• • • • • • •

• • • • • • •

What would happen to you if you get scared half to death twice? ☺

Eleanor Roosevelt

• • • • • • •

• • • • • • •

If practice makes perfect but
nobody is perfect, then why
practice?

George Washington

Don't let success go to your head
nor let failure go to your heart.

Billy Graham

• • • • • • •

• • • • • • •

Tact is the art of making a point without making an enemy.

Sir Isaac Newton

• • • • • • •

• • • • • • •

So are you going out tonight?

Sure

Where are you going?

Club B.E.D. with DJ Pillow ☺

• • • • • • •

• • • • • • •

Buy and wear hair
industry T-shirts

• • • • • • •

• • • • • • •

Self expression is the purest form of individuality. Don't ever be afraid to reveal it. It's what makes you, you.

Mary
In Behindthechair.com/
onpaper culture 2009

• • • • • • •

No word in the English
language rhymes
with orange, month,
silver, purple or
discombobulate.

• • • • • • •

Our eyes are always the
same size from birth, but
our nose and ears never
stop growing.

• • • • • • •

Be kind, for everyone you meet is fighting a hard battle.

Plato

● ● ● ● ● ● ●

Remember that you're unique – just like everyone else.

Sir Isaac Newton

● ● ● ● ● ● ●

• • • • • • •

Overnight success takes 15 years

Eddie Cantor

• • • • • • •

• • • • • • •

Bad habits are like a comfortable bed- easy to get into, but hard to get out of.

Winston Churchill

• • • • • • •

• • • • • • •

Vogue is still a great style magazine

• • • • • • •

• • • • • • •

If you think nobody cares, try missing

a payment.

Philip Dormer Stanhop

• • • • • • •

Why don't they make the whole plane out of that BLACK BOX stuff?

Steven Wright

• • • • • • •

Sign seen in salon:
Unsupervised   children
will be given sugar and a
free puppy. ☺

• • • • • • •

• • • • • • •

Be humble or you'll stumble.

Dwight Moody

• • • • • • •

• • • • • • •

Do the math –

1 hair cut $55.

Add a color for $80

Add a purification treatment $10

Add a conditioning treatment $20

Add the commission of retail $3

Add gratuity of 20% for good service of $33.60

That = $201.60

Do that 5 times in a week = $1,008.

• • • • • • •

• • • • • • •

Check out
Mahogany Hair dressing
UK

• • • • • • •

• • • • • • •

The secret to making progress "Pray with your feet moving! Because Faith without works is dead"

Anthony Robbins

• • • • • • •

To all hair stylist--

The trouble with being punctual to your first appointment is that there is no one there to appreciate it.

Franklin P. Jones

● ● ● ● ● ● ●

When your mother is angry at your
father don't let her brush your hair.

Walt Meloon

● ● ● ● ● ● ●

· · · · · · ·

Know your culture

Salon owners know this--

There is a leader in your salon.

If it is not you, make sure you

know who it is.

If you don't know for sure,

Its definitely not you.

Alfredo Kierszman

· · · · · · ·

• • • • • • •

Hire people smarter than you are

and then get out of their way.

Howard Schultz

• • • • • • •

• • • • • • •

Salon owners trust your stylists
until they give you a
reason not too.
Stylists never talk ill of the salon
owners until they give you
a reason too.

Alfredo Kierszman

• • • • • • •

• • • • • • •

When the student is ready the teacher will arrive.

Wax on Wax off

(My wife made me...lol)

• • • • • • •

You know what I hate?

Indian givers

No, I take that back.

Emo Philips

• • • • • • •

You make the world a better place by making yourself a better person.

Scott Sorrell

• • • • • • •

• • • • • • •

Have style please
Dress on purpose

(Don't get caught @ peopleofwalmart.com)

• • • • • • •

Stylist let's work together

1 Million Stylist Together

1 Cure

To Cure Blonde-orexia

Together we can do it.

• • • • • • •

The Head

Perimeter – Responsible for length

Plane – Flat portion of the head, bulk of hair / direction occurs

Crown – Cowlicks, growth patterns, height

Top section – In this section most effects occur for different facial shapes. Most movement of the hair color occurs in this section creating special effects.

• • • • • • •

• • • • • • •

"The quick brown fox jumps over
the lazy dog"
The preceding sentence uses every
letter of the alphabet.

• • • • • • •

• • • • • • •

Clients or Stylists you decide

We see them come. We see them go.

Some are fast. And some are slow.

Some are high. And some are low.

Not one of them is like another.

Don't ask us why. Go ask your mother.

Dr. Seuss

• • • • • • •

• • • • • • •

You Might be a Redneck if You think loading the dishwasher means getting your wife drunk. You think King of the Hill, is a reality show based on your life story. Go Country >!< ☺

Jeff Foxworthy

• • • • • • •

● ● ● ● ● ● ●

Hair has great social significance

for human beings. It can grow on most areas

of the human body, except on the palms of

the hands and the soles of the feet (among

other areas), but hair is most noticeable

in most people in a small number of areas,

which are also the ones that are most

commonly trimmed, plucked, or shaved. These

include the face, nose, ears, head, eyebrows,

eyelashes, legs and armpits, as well as the pubic

region. The highly visible differences between

male and female body and facial hair are a

notable secondary sex characteristic.

● ● ● ● ● ● ●

• • • • • • •
Hair as indicator

Healthy hair indicates health and youth (important in evolutionary biology). Hair color and texture can be a sign of ethnic ancestry. Facial hair is a sign of puberty in men. White hair is a sign of age or genetics, which can be concealed with hair dye. Male pattern baldness is a sign of age, which can be concealed with a toupee, hats or religious/cultural adornments. Although drugs and medical procedures exist for the treatment of baldness, many balding men simply shave their heads.

• • • • • • •

● ● ● ● ● ● ●

Some Tips and Bits from
the Human Performance Institute

www.CorporateAthlete.com

Managing energy, not time, is the key to extraordinary results.

* Eat breakfast everyday

* Never go longer then 4 hours without food; eat light, eat often

* Eat no more then 5 handfuls of food per meal

* Ideal meals contain both carbohydrates and protein

* Snacks should be low glycemic

* In order to maximize energy stop eating when you
  feel satisfied not full

* Drink water regularly throughout the day

* Go to bed and wake up at the same time everyday

* Get 7 to 8 hours of sleep each night

● ● ● ● ● ● ●

* Do some form of physical activity daily
  (even if you have a physical job)

* Exercise at a moderate to high intensity to
  maximize the workout

* Do at least 2 cardiovascular interval
  workouts per week.

* Think quality, not quantity, to maximize
  your work out

* Some exercise is better than nothing at all

• • • • • • •

She wants her hair colored back
to her original color.
The problem is, remembering
what that color is. ☺

• • • • • • •

● ● ● ● ● ● ●

Her hair is straight
It's her head that's wavy

● ● ● ● ● ● ●

Know the answer to these questions. For some strange reason clients still ask.

1. Why does my gray come back so quickly? Answer: Because your hair does not stop growing when we color it. Sorry

2. How long will it take for my short hair to grow to the middle of my back? Answer: Well, if hair grows at an average of 1/2 inch per month that = 6 inches per year more or less.

3. How many hairs is normal hair loss? Answer: The average daily hair loss is between 100 and 200 hairs.

● ● ● ● ● ● ●

4. Does Rogaine and medicines like that work?

Answer: Yes

5. What causes hair loss in men and women?

This one you'll just have to look up. It's not that I don't know. I just don't feel like writing it out.

You still should know the answer...lol

• • • • • • •

...Just Kidding

Hair Loss in women

Although there are many conditions, diseases, and hair care practices that can result in female thinning hair and excessive hair loss, hereditary hair loss accounts for 95% of all women with hair loss. The pattern is different than men and is more diffuse. Hair loss can also be a symptom of stress, pregnancy, and the taking of certain medications.

• • • • • • •

• • • • • • •

Hair Loss in Men

By far the most common cause of hair loss in men is androgenetic alopecia, also referred to as "male pattern" or "common" baldness. It is caused by the effects of the male hormone dihydrotestosterone (DHT) on genetically susceptible scalp hair follicles. This sensitivity to DHT is present mainly in hair follicles that reside in the front, top, and crown of the scalp (rather than the back and sides) producing a characteristic and easily identifiable pattern. It is frequently stated that "hair loss comes from the mother's side of the family." The truth is that the condition can be inherited from either parent. However, recent research

• • • • • • •

• • • • • • •

suggests that the situation may be a bit more complex than was originally thought. Factors on the x-chromosome have been shown to influence hair loss, making the inheritance from the maternal side of the family slightly more important than the paternal one (Markus Nothen, 2005).

• • • • • • •

• • • • • • •

Main Entry: 1or•gan•ic

Pronunciation: \or-ga-nik\

Function: adjective

Of, relating to, or arising in a bodily organ;
Affecting the structure of the organism; Of,
relating to, or derived from living organisms.
Of, relating to, yielding, or involving the use of
food produced with the use of feed or fertilizer
of plant or animal origin without employment
of chemically formulated fertilizers, growth
stimulants, antibiotics, or pesticides; Forming an
integral element of a whole rather than organic
parts of the action having systematic coordination
of parts an organic whole developing in the
manner of a living plant or animal

Source Web Dictionary

• • • • • • •

• • • • • • •

In Short – it is far from it - if not close to impossible to have a truly organic hair care product. Why? Because the product would have to be placed in a refrigerator to stay fresh and would only last a few days. To go further regarding this: Yes in the U.S. you can call something organic if a small % of the ingredients in the product is derivatives of an organic source. So now you know.

• • • • • • •

• • • • • • •

pH - (potential of hydrogen)
A measure of the acidity or alkalinity of a solution, numerically equal to 7 for neutral solutions, increasing with increasing alkalinity and decreasing with increasing acidity. The pH scale commonly in use ranges from 0 to 14.

Source Web Dictionary

So clients and stylist love to ask: "Is that product pH-balanced? Kind of a silly question, because if it were not, it would be unstable, and instability in a shampoo = activity which = a reaction that is uncontrollable which =? Yeah exactly. All products in a liquid form have a pH. The proper question then becomes what is the pH of a product? If you like the answer, then use the product. On the other hand liking the answer will solely depend on what you want the product to perform; if you need the product to close the cuticle or help you in opening the cuticle. It becomes your call.

• • • • • • •

● ● ● ● ● ● ●

A few more facts about us

Cosmetology as an academic discipline

The University of Osnabrück, Germany, has established the course "Cosmetology" in the faculty of human sciences as a scientific branch of health sciences. A Bachelors degree, Dr. Rer. Nat. say must be obtained.

The 2003 NACCAS Job Demand Survey suggests that there is a shortage of salon professionals in the working world, so cosmetologists and salon professionals have increased earning power.

● ● ● ● ● ● ●

• • • • • • •

Social Media
Step By Step

This is a fictional guide for a salon that does not exist. (Key Source is A Professional's Guide to Social Media by Joel Goldstein.)

This guide will instruct you on the order in which to set up and progress your Social Media marketing campaign in order to project a professional image for optimum efficiency.

•Create the business name: Angel Gio Salon (or your name that identifies you, ex. Hair4U)

Check with your governmental agency for the DBA and the use of the name. (In Florida, you need to go to www.sunbiz.org and apply there)

•Create a username: angelgio
Try to keep uniformity throughout all your social media platforms

• • • • • • •

• • • • • • •

●Create a logo: **Angel Gio Salon**
Make sure you have a vector graphic so it is scalable and you can use it on all your marketing.
Do not make it ambiguous

●Take a professional profile picture that reflects your style and persona. Keep it universal throughout all of your social networks.

●Come up with a pertinent quote: *Hers and His looks for everyday style.*
Put this quote in all your socials platforms.

●Buy a domain name and hosting. I like to use Go Daddy and create your website; for ex. www.angelgiosalon.com

●Set up a professional email account: Angelique@angelgiosalon.com
Set up a signature for all outgoing emails that includes your contact information as well as all your social platform profile links.

• • • • • • •

● ● ● ● ● ● ●

•If you have employees that will also be contributors, have them create usernames and e-mails such as Giovanni@angelgiosalon. (Please note that this would be good for commission employees as well as booth rental because it creates a unified image of the salon, which is great for all of your marketing)

•Put a link to your domain name on all your social networks

•If you cannot afford hosting, purchase a domain name for $10 a year and have it forwarded to your Blogger Blog or there are various website that will host you for free for ex. www.weebly.com. This is good for a beginning site as you become savvier you would want to upgrade.

At this time, you would want a professional to create a website for you. As you would tell your clients, not to do their highlights, lowlights and keratin treatment themselves. :)

● ● ● ● ● ● ●

• • • • • • •

•Use Wordpress as the content management system and implement auto posting plugins so each post is automatically posted on your socials networks.

•Create a sub domain for a blog; ex. www. blog.angelgiosalon.com

•Join an email marketing site such as Aweber or Constant Contact

•Set up a newsletter sign up form. Put the form on all your social platforms that allows you to. Set up 5 emails under the auto responder. They can be tutorials or instructional guides.

•Join Facebook

•Create personal profiles with all you business information readily available.

•Create groups, fan pages, Etc.

•Create a business page for you company ask people to become fans

• • • • • • •

• • • • • • •

•Join LinkedIn

•Do sign up to as many social sites a you can manage. Key word – manage :)

•Keep a sign up sheet at your station or at the front desk and encourage clients to be a part of the online conversations.

•Do join flicker – this will become an online portfolio for you

•Join YouTube and add videos of you working or of relevant work. Find other people in the industry and comment on their videos with a link back to yours.
Put links to your youtube profile on other social networks

•Join myspace and put up a professional profile (while it last. It still was #1 in 2009.)

• • • • • • •

● ● ● ● ● ● ●

•Join Digg.com
Post a Digg button on each blog page you post. Make sure you Digg your own post. (Not a joke) lol
Become active in the Digg community and Digg other peoples pages.

•Create a Blog on Blogger

Use your domain name to forward to this website if you do not have a website of your own. If you do, add the link from your site to your blog.

•Fill out all of your contact information on the "About" page so people can find you if they would like to do business.

•Join Ping.fm
Link as many social sites to as you can
This way you can post to all or some of your socials to update your Status.

● ● ● ● ● ● ●

• • • • • • •

Remember that there are other sites for this but I like Ping it just to easy.

•Lastly, to manage your top social networks or blogs join and use Hootsuite.com

Let me simplify this so you see it. Every time you post something online the whole world can see it. If someone is asking a question and you are the one giving the answers in your field, then you become to them the credible source and the authority. If they are local to you or have a need to use your product and/or service you offer, chances are they will come to your business.

So you post to get your product and service seen by others, kind of like a billboard on the side of a highway with many passing by. Many will not see your sign, many will, some may even like it enough to comment on it, and some will pull off the highway to go shopping in your store. Excuse the cliché, but yes, you are a part of the information super highway.

• • • • • • •

• • • • • • •

You are ready so go and have fun!

I know all this sounds like a lot of work, but chances are, you are doing all of, if not part of this stuff already. The difference is that in this way and by using this guide, you will be focused on your business and you will see results.

It may seem overwhelming and it is. So take it in small bites. You can spend and may spend hours putting together this stuff in the beginning, but once it is set up it becomes about managing and that may take an hour a week more or less depending on your zeal. It is all worth it though, do it now and don't be left behind, because, social media isn't going away, I promise.

• • • • • • •

● ● ● ● ● ● ●

Pings

I am giving you examples of pings and tweets, they are not all mine, but it is pings like the once that follow and many more that have taken my site from being visited by 2 or 3 people per day to 10, 15, and sometimes more per day. Oh yeah and my service bookings and retail sales have doubled. Remember they come across as blurbs of words to the reader. But say the right thing, catch someone's attention, and you have a friend or follower. Then reel them in and you have a client. Note: I don't always talk about me, but I always refer them back to me via my web address.

www.hairbyalfredo.com :)

● ● ● ● ● ● ●

• • • • • • •

Mondays are my Sundays and I'm enjoying a day off. I'm getting mentally ready to do some great hair tomorrow. www.HairByAlfredo.com

I'm hair for you. >!< www.HairByAlfredo. com

• • • • • • •

@typefaster I think you're right. I will be sure to mention the senior's discount! 12:08 PM Mar 24th via web in reply to typefaster

Exciting salon news... as of April 1 there will be not one, but two hairstylists working at Tangles Hair Design! www. TanglesHairDesign.ca

Katherine Heigl is now a brunette! Shocking. http://www.stylelist.com/2010/03/09/ katherine-heigl-hair-blonde-brown-dark/

Cleanse. Condition. Correct. Create. with Abba Pure Haircare Products. Yours free with a color. http://tinyurl.com/yz77oec

• • • • • • •

Hmm… just had a hair brained idea. Do more hair….lol www.HairByAlfredo.com

Take my advice. I'm not using it. The only thing constant is change

Ralph Waldo Emerson

Thank you, Shahn Douglas

• • • • • • •

● ● ● ● ● ● ●

Like that T-shirt

"Only action gives life strength. Only moderation gives it charm." >!<

www.HairByAlfredo.com

Beautiful hair starts with Alfredo :)

www.HairByAlfredo.com

● ● ● ● ● ● ●

• • • • • • •

Anyone want a free Glaze + blowout monday 9am with one of our fabulous educators Reply here call 2122427786x306 aaron@arrojocosmetology.com

twistscissors

i'm tring to start my own clean hair care line. if anyone has any suggestions or places to buy all natural products please let me know!

ok, so im on my last stretch for my green hair care line but i still havent thought of a name. if you got a good one let me know!

• • • • • • •

• • • • • • •

"Great quality is related to great design; you rarely get one without the other" Giorgio Armani :) www.HairByAlfredo.com

Alfredo; Because Creativity Requires Brilliance www.HairByAlfredo.com

• • • • • • •

• • • • • • •

Checking out "Extensions by Alfredo" on

www.HairByAlfredo.com

Join   Orlando's   own   Style   Network

by Alfredo your Personal Style www.

HairByAlfredo.com

• • • • • • •

• • • • • • •

Check out celebrity secrets and fashion advice from a Celebrity Stylist @ www.HairByAlfredo.com

FitFullForce

"Movement is a medicine for creating change ina person's physical, emotional, and mental state."

Excited about Commit2Fit! Information on how u can participate and raise donations 4 Relay coming soon 2 my website

Tilapia pic added to Get Inspired on www.fitfullforce.com

• • • • • • •

• • • • • • •

The golden rule to get fit & lean: Eat clean and train smart! So, Ingest high quality nutrients and train your muscles w/ heavy resistance!

FitFullForce: Baby spinach, artichoke hearts, strawberries, drizzled with raspberry vineg. Recipe coming to soon www.fitfullforce.com

• • • • • • •

• • • • • • •

tonyrobbins

"The world makes way for the man who knows where he is going." Ralph Waldo Emerson happy easter everyone!

U are now at a crossroads. This is your opportunity 2 make the most important decision you will ever make. who are U now? Who will u become?

Fear has only 2 causes:the thought of losing what U have or the thought of not getting what U want. Who U become as a soul is immutable 5:09 PM Mar 24th via TweetDeck

• • • • • • •

• • • • • • •

Thank you, Modern Salon, and welcome –

Now you're a hair above the rest for joining

my style network @ www.HairByAlfredo.

com

• • • • • • •

● ● ● ● ● ● ●

My friend and colleague Stephen Soto, Educational Manager for Alfaparf Milano, reminded me of an awesome truth and responsibility we as licensed Cosmetologist have. Some of us have forgotten or take it for granted.

You see we can all style hair and that's the easy part of our job for the most part, but what we can never forget is our POWER OF TOUCH.

"We are just 1 of a total of 5 industries that actually have a license to touch."

He is right and in these modern days with the Internet and its Pings and Tweets many faces and mobile devices, we still retain the civility

● ● ● ● ● ● ●

• • • • • • •

and ability to heal, bring joy, and trigger

the release of brain endorphins to make

Others Happy

Just by our Touch.

• • • • • • •

Wow, You Are AMAZING.

www.eatpaintsweat.com

• • • • • • •

Thank you.
Now you are a hair above the rest.

For more information about anything in this book that you can't find online, email me at fringefirst@gmail. com or befriend me or follow me or tweet me or text me or just call me at 407-461-7887.

• • • • • • •

- - - - - - -

Sites of interest

www.HairByAlfredo.com

www.YouTube.com

www.People.com

www.ExpertVillage.com

www.Professionals-Guide.com

www.Instyle.com

www.Salontoday.com

www.Bravotv.com

www.BehindTheChair.com

www.FitFullForce.com

www.eatpainsweat.com

www.flickr.com

- - - - - - -

• • • • • • •

Special thanks and sources of inspirations and information to

Joel Goldstein of www.PeerMarketingGroup. com

Tom Dispense Author /Colorist – Hair 296 Facts and tip to better hair coloring

David H. Walker, Jr. – Author Sin qua Nuns Some of Life's Essentials (and other stuff, too)

Stephen Soto, Artistic Director at Essentials Salon & Spa – www.essentials-spa.com and Educational Manager, Alfaparf Milano

The World of Color Technical Book – Alfaparf Milano

The Human Performance Institute

& Joyce Fowlkes for her editorial support.

• • • • • • •

• • • • • • •

Key terms in social media and networking

From http://socialmedia.wikispaces.com/
AZ+of+social+media

Aggregation is the process of gathering and remixing content from blogs and other websites that provide RSS feeds. The results may be displayed in an aggregator website like Bloglines, or directly on your desktop using software often also called a newsreader.

Authenticity is the sense that something or someone is "real". Blogs enable people to publish content, and engage in conversations, that show their interests and values, and so help develop an authentic voice online.

Blogs are websites with dated items of content in reverse chronological order, self-published by bloggers. Items – sometimes called posts - may have keyword tags associated with them, are usually available as feeds, and often allow commenting.

Bookmarking is saving the address of a website or item of content, either in your brower, or on a social bookmarking

• • • • • • •

site like del.icio.us. If you add tags, others can easily use your research too

Browser is the tool used to view websites, and access all the content available there onscreen or by downloading. Browsers may also be used to upload or otherwise contribute content to a blog or other website.

Bulletin boards were the early vehicles for online collaboration, where users connected with a central computer to post and read email-like messages. They were the electronic equivalent of public notice boards. The term is still used for forums.

Chat is interaction on a web site, with a number of people adding text items one after the other into the same space at (almost) the same time. A place for chat – chat room – differs from a forum because conversations happen in "real time", rather as they do face to face.

Collaboration: social media tools from email lists to virtual worlds offer enormous scope for collaboration. Low-risk

• • • • • • •

activities like commenting, social bookmarking, chatting and blogging help develop the trust necessary for collaboration.

Commitment: the "social" aspect of social media means that tools are most useful when other people commit to using them too. Commitment will depend on people's degree of interest in a subject, capability online, preparedness to share with others, degree of comfort in a new place, as well as the usability of the site or tool.

Online communities are groups of people communicating mainly through the Internet. They may simply have a shared interest to talk about ... or more formally learn from each other and find solutions as a Community of Practice. Online communities may use email lists or forums, where content is centralised. Communities may also emerge from conversations around or between bloggers.

Content is used here to describe text, pictures, video and any other meaningful material that is on the Internet.

Control: social networking is difficult to control because if

• • • • • • •

• • • • • • •

people can't say something in one place they can blog or comment elsewhere. That can be challenging for hierarchical organisations used to centrally-managed websites.

Conversation through blogging, commenting or contributing to forums is the currency of social networking.

Copyright: sharing through social media is enhanced by attaching a Creative Commons license specifying, for example, that content may be re-used with attribution, provided that a similar license is then attached by the new author.

Crowdsourcing refers to harnessing the skills and enthusiasm of those outside an organisation who are prepared to volunteer their time contributing content and solving problems.

Culture: social media only works well in a culture of openness, where people are prepared to share. For that reason, commitment and attitude are as important as tools.

• • • • • • •

• • • • • • •

Download is to retrieve a file or other content from an Internet site to your computer or other device. See Upload.

Email lists, or groups, are important networking tools offering the facility to "starburst" a message from a central postbox to any number of subscribers, and for them to respond. Lists usually also offer a facility for reading and replying through a web page - so they can also operate like forums.

Face-to-face (f2) is used to describe people meeting offline. While social media may reduce the need to meet, direct contact gives far more clues, quickly, about a person than you can get online. Online interaction is likely to be richer after f2f meetings.

Feeds are the means by which you can read, view or listen to items from blogs and other RSS-enabled sites without visiting the site, by subscribing and using an aggregator or newsreader. Feeds contain the content of an item and any associated tags without the design or structure of a web page.

• • • • • • •

● ● ● ● ● ● ●

Forums are discussion areas on websites, where people can post messages or comment on existing messages asynchronously – that is, independently of time or place time. Chat is the synchronous equivalent.

Groups are collections of individuals with some sense of unity through their activities, interests or values. They are bounded: you are in a group, or not. They differ in this from networks, which are dispersed, and defined by nodes and connections.

Instant messaging (IM) is chat with one other person.

Links are the highlighted text or images that, when clicked, jump you from one web page or item of content to another. Bloggers use links a lot when writing, to reference their own or other content.

Lurkers are people who read but don't contribute or add comments to forums. The one per cent rule-of-thumb suggests about one per cent of people contribute new content to an online community, another nine percent comment, and the rest lurk. However, this may not be a passive role because content read on forums may spark interaction elsewhere.

● ● ● ● ● ● ●

• • • • • • •

Membership involves belonging to a group. Networking can offer some of the benefits of group membership, without the need for as much central co-ordination. A rise in networking may present challenges for organisations who depend on membership for funds or to demonstrate their credibility.

Networks are structures defined by nodes and the connections between them. In social networks the nodes are people, and the connections are the relationships that they have. Networking is the process by which you develop and strengthen those relationships.

Newsreader See aggregator.

Online means being connected to the Internet, and also being there in the sense of reading or producing content.

Offline means not online, that is, not connected to the Internet. It may refer to an unconnected computer, or activities taking place without the benefit (or perhaps distraction) of a connection.

• • • • • • •

● ● ● ● ● ● ●

Openness is being prepared to share and collaborate – something aided by social media. Open source software - developed collaboratively with few constraints on its use - is a technical example. In order to be open online you may offer share-alike copyright licenses, and you may tag content and link generously to other people's content. This demonstrates open source thinking.

Peer to peer refers to direct interaction between two people in a network. In that network, each peer will be connected to other peers, opening the opportunity for further sharing and learning.

Platform is the framework or system within which tools work. That platform may be as broad as mobile telephony, or as narrow as a piece of software that has different modules like blogs, forums, and wikis in a suite of tools. As more and more tools operate "out there" on the web, rather than on your desktop, people refer to "the Internet as the platform.

Podcast is audio or video content that can be downloaded automatically through a subscription to a website so you can view or listen offline.

● ● ● ● ● ● ●

●　●　●　●　●　●　●

Profiles are the information that you provide about yourself when signing up for a social networking site. As well as a picture and basic information, this may include your personal and business interests, a "blurb" about yourself, and tags to help people search for like-minded people.

Remixing: social media offers the possibility of taking different items of content, identified by tags and published through feeds, and combining them in different ways. You can do this with other people's content if they add an appropriate copyright license.

Roles: parties need hosting, committees need chairing, working groups may need facilitation. Online networks and communities need support from people who may be called, for example, technology stewards or network weavers. Champions are the core group of enthusiasts you need to start a community.

RSS is short for Really Simple Syndication. This allows you to subscribe to content on blogs and other social media and have it delivered to you through a feed.

●　●　●　●　●　●　●

● ● ● ● ● ● ●

Searching for information on the Net is done using a search engine, of which Google is the best known. Specialist search engines like Technorati concentrate on blogs. As well as searching by word or phrase you can search on tags, and so find content others have keyworded.

Sharing is offering other people the use of your text, images, video, bookmarks or other content by adding tags, and applying copyright licenses that encourage use of content.

Social media is a terms for the tools and platforms people use to publish, converse and share content online. The tools include blogs, wikis, podcasts, and sites to share photos and bookmarks.

Social networking sites are online places where users can create a profile for themselves, and then socialise with others using a range of social media tools including blogs, video, images, tagging, lists of friends, forums and messaging.

Stories, as well as conversations, are a strong theme in blogging. Anecdotes, bits of gossip and longer narratives

● ● ● ● ● ● ●

• • • • • • •

work particularly well on blogs if they have a personal angle. It helps others get to know the blogger - and helps the blogger find and extend their voice.

Subscribing is the process of adding an RSS feed to your aggregator or newsreader. It's the online equivalent of signing up for a magazine, but usually free.

Tags are keywords attached to a blog post, bookmark, photo or other item of content so you and others can find them easily through searches and aggregation.

Terms of services are the basis on which you agree to use a forum or other web-based place for creating or sharing content. Check before agreeing what rights the site owners may claim over your content.

Threads are strands of conversation. On an email list or web forum they will be defined by messages that use the use the same subject. On blogs they are less clearly defined, but emerge through comments and trackbacks.

Tool is used here as shorthand for a software applications

• • • • • • •

on your computer, and also for applications that are Web-based.

Trackback: some blogs provide a facility for other bloggers to leave a calling card automatically, instead of commenting. Blogger A may write on blog A about an item on blogger B's site, and through the trackback facility leave a link on B's site back to A. The collection of comments and trackbacks on a site facilitates conversations.

Transparency: Enhancing searching, sharing, self-publish and commenting across networks makes it easier to find out what's going on in any situation where there is online activity.

Upload is to transfer a file or other content from your computer to an Internet site.

User generated content is text, photos and other material produced by people who previously just consumed. See content.

Virtual worlds are online places like Second Life, where

● ● ● ● ● ● ●

you can create a representation of yourself (an avatar) and socialise with other residents. Basic activity is free, but you can buy currency (using real money) in order to purchase land and trade with other residents. Second Life is being used by some voluntary organisations to run discussions, virtual events and fundraising.

Voice over Internet Protocol (VOIP) enables you to use a computer or other Internet device for phone calls without additional charge.

Web 2.0 is a term coined by O'Reilly Media in 2004 to describe blogs, wikis, social networking sites and other Internet-based services that emphasise collaboration and sharing, rather than less interactive publishing (Web 1.0). It is associated with the idea of the Internet as platform.

A **wiki** is a web page - or set of pages - that can be edited collaboratively. The best known example is wikipedia, an encyclopedia created by thousands of contributors across the world. Once people have appropriate permissions - set by the wiki owner - they can create pages and/ or add to and alter existing pages.

● ● ● ● ● ● ●